THE SCIENCE OF HISTORY

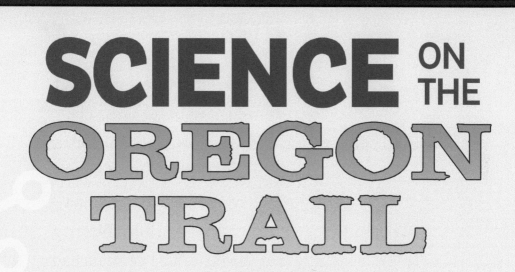

SCIENCE ON THE
OREGON
TRAIL

by Tammy Enz

CAPSTONE PRESS
a capstone imprint

Capstone Captivate is published by Capstone Press,
an imprint of Capstone.
1710 Roe Crest Drive
North Mankato, Minnesota 56003
www.capstonepub.com

Library of Congress Cataloging-in-Publication Data
Names: Enz, Tammy, author.
Title: Science on the Oregon Trail / by Tammy Enz.
Description: North Mankato, Minnesota : Capstone Press, an imprint of Capstone, [2021] | Series: The science of history | Includes bibliographical references and index. | Audience: Ages 8-11 | Audience: Grades 4-6 | Summary: "You may have heard of the Oregon Trail. In the 1840s, more than 5,000 people traveled the Oregon Trail, hoping for a better life. But did you know that science played a big role in this epic journey? Learn how covered wagons were engineered. Find out how food was preserved and diseases were treated along the trail. And discover how modern technology is helping us learn even more about this time in history"-- Provided by publisher. Identifiers: LCCN 2021002791 (print) | LCCN 2021002792 (ebook) | ISBN 9781496695420 (library binding) | ISBN 9781496696915 (paperback) | ISBN 9781977159175 (eBook PDF) | ISBN 9781977159274 (Kindle edition) Subjects: LCSH: Transportation engineering--West (U.S.)--History--19th century--Juvenile literature. | Oregon National Historic Trail--History--19th century--Juvenile literature. | Frontier and pioneer life--West (U.S.)--History--19th century--Juvenile literature. | Overland journeys to the Pacific--History--19th century--Juvenile literature. Classification: LCC TA1023.6 .E59 2021 (print) | LCC TA1023.6 (ebook) | DDC 978/.02--dc23 LC record available at https://lccn.loc.gov/2021002791 LC ebook record available at https://lccn.loc.gov/2021002792

Editorial Credits
Editors, Angie Kaelberer and Aaron Sautter; Designer, Heidi Thompson; Media Researcher, Svetlana Zhurkin; Production Specialist, Kathy McColley

Image Credits
Bridgeman Images: © Look and Learn, 30; Capstone: 11, 14; iStockphoto: ilbusca, 21, stocksnapper, 12, whitemay, 41; Library of Congress: 16; North Wind Picture Archives: 15, 19, 20, 42, Nancy Carter, 29; Scotts Bluff National Monument: William Henry Jackson Collection, cover (bottom), 1 (top), 5, 25 (top), 45; Shutterstock: Andriy Blokhin, 25 (bottom), Anna Kutukova, 43 (tree), Arthur Villator, 13, ButtermilkgirlVirginia, 17, Designua, 37, Djomas, 43 (men), Everett Collection, 33, 39, Greenni, 31, KamimiArt (design element), 1 (bottom) and throughout, Marla Margarla, 35, Minerva Studio, 27, Morphart Creation, 23, rdonar, cover (top), 10, Singha Songsak P, 9, StudioKampOC, 36, Tancha, 43 (wagon), VectorMine, 7; XNR Productions: 6

TABLE OF CONTENTS

Words in **bold** text are included in the glossary.

CHAPTER 1

WAGONS HO!

In the early 1800s, most people in the United States lived in the East. The land west of the Mississippi River was mostly unsettled. But the West Coast offered rich farmland and mild weather. There was even the chance of finding gold.

However, the journey west seemed impossible. It meant traveling thousands of miles over deserts and mountains. There were no roads, hotels, or stores to help travelers on their journey.

Yet, the challenges didn't stop daring explorers who blazed a path to the West. They spoke of the riches on the West Coast. Soon travelers began packing wagons and heading toward the Oregon Territory. The route they followed was called the Oregon Trail.

The Oregon Trail pioneers were a brave group. They battled bad weather and disease. They suffered many hardships as they traveled. They had little to no scientific knowledge. But science shaped their trip more than most would know.

Fact

From the 1840s through the 1860s, about 300,000 to 500,000 people traveled the Oregon Trail.

DESERTS TO FARMLANDS

The Oregon Trail began in Independence, Missouri. It ended in Oregon City, Oregon. Traveling the 2,000-mile (3,218-kilometer) distance with wagons and cattle was slow. Settlers first crossed the open plains that were part of the Louisiana Purchase in 1803. They then had to search for water and food in dry deserts. Finally, they made the dangerous crossing over the mountains.

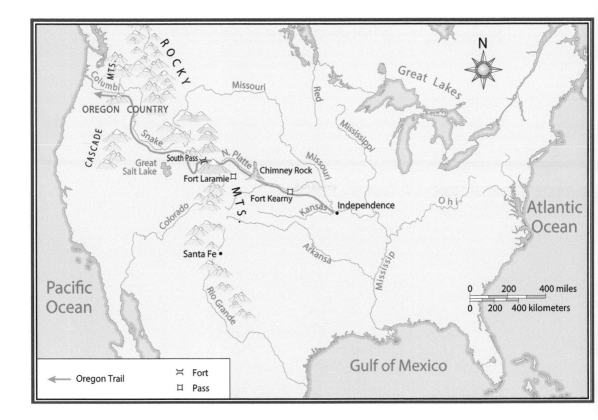

On the west coast, moist ocean air creates lush farmlands on the west side of mountain ranges. But the mountains create a rain shadow that causes desertlike conditions on the east side. As warm, wet air moves in from the Pacific Ocean, it rises over the Sierra Nevada mountains. The air cools and forms clouds, which dump rain and snow on the west side. When the air moves to the east side, its moisture is gone. The area east of the mountains gets very little rainfall and is often a hot, dry desert.

Rain Shadows

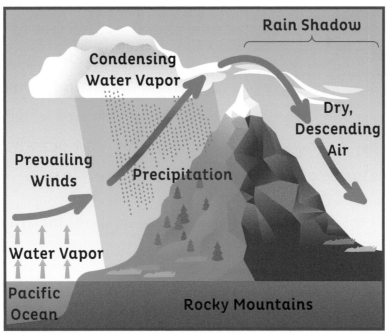

7

CHAPTER 2

PACKING UP

Oregon Trail settlers traveled in wagons called prairie schooners. Enough food was packed in the schooner to last for several months. Tools and supplies for a new life out west were crammed in as well. It all needed protection from the hot sun and prairie storms.

A prairie schooner was a basic farm wagon with a canvas top. Tough, long-lasting canvas is made from tightly woven cotton. To make the canvas waterproof, settlers rubbed it with linseed oil from flax plants. Oil **molecules** and water molecules repel each other. Oiled canvas sheds away water.

Fact

The prairie schooner wagon was named after a sailboat called a schooner. People thought the white canvas tops looked like sailboats as they moved through the tall prairie grasses.

To form the wagon tops, settlers stretched oiled canvas over bent wooden ribs. Wagon builders bent and shaped hickory wood by steaming it. Steaming the wood loosened the lignin in the wood cells. Lignin is an organic **polymer** that binds wood cells together. It's flexible when heated. When cooled, lignin hardens to hold the new shape.

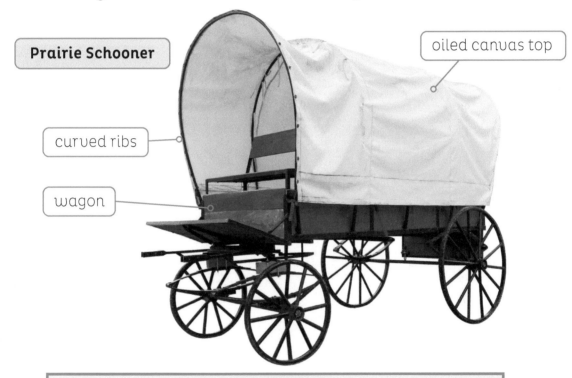

Prairie Schooner

oiled canvas top

curved ribs

wagon

Bumpy Ride

A suspension system is a flexible system between a vehicle's wheels and frame. It includes springs and shock absorbers. These parts absorb bumps and help provide a smooth ride. But wagons didn't have suspension systems. Most settlers chose to walk beside their wagons. It was more comfortable than the rough, bumpy ride inside their wagons.

SHAPING METAL

Most settlers were good at making and fixing things. But needed help with one thing. Blacksmiths had the tools and knowledge to work with metal. Blacksmiths shaped iron to make wagon wheel rims. They also made horseshoes. These U-shaped metal plates protected horses' feet on rough terrain.

Shaping iron and other metals involves very high temperatures—up to 2,000 degrees Fahrenheit (1,093 degrees Celsius). Getting metal that hot requires a forge. A forge is like a big oven. It burns coal so hot that it becomes almost pure carbon. Carbon is a basic **element**.

Blacksmiths heated iron in hot forges to make horseshoes and other metal objects.

A blacksmith used a device called a bellows to force oxygen into the super-hot carbon. Oxygen causes the carbon to burn even hotter. The chemical reaction between the carbon and oxygen is called combustion. More oxygen means more combustion and a hotter flame. Iron was heated until it glowed orange. Then it was soft enough for the blacksmith to pound into shape.

How Combustion Works

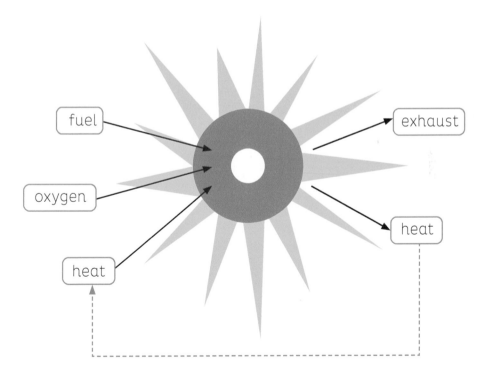

PRESERVING FOOD

Food was one of the settlers' most important needs. They could hunt bison and other animals as they traveled. But other foods had to be packed and brought in their wagons. The pioneers had no way to keep food cold. Without refrigeration, food spoils quickly. In the 1800s, the best way to store fruits, vegetables, and other foods was to dry them.

Pioneers took hundreds of pounds of food with them on their journey, including sacks of cornmeal, dried beans, rice, potatoes, and preserved meat.

Drying food prevents the biggest cause of food spoilage—bacteria. Bacteria are **microorganisms**. They break down food for nutrients. As bacteria break down food, it begins to rot. But bacteria need moisture to do their work. The pioneers dried their food to remove water. Setting food out in the hot sun for a day or two usually dried it enough to make it safe.

Meats like ham or bacon were preserved with salt curing. Salt draws water out of cells. Soaking meat in salty water or rubbing it with salt helped preserve it. Travelers sometimes packed bacon in barrels of bran, which is the hard outer layer of grains such as oats. Packing bacon this way helped keep the bacon fat from melting in the hot sun.

Salt was often used to preserve meat. The salt helped remove moisture and kept bacteria from spoiling the meat.

MAKING SOAP

Walking on dusty trails and cooking over campfires made staying clean a real chore. But keeping clean is an important part of staying healthy. That meant packing soap—lots of it.

Dirt and disease-causing germs cling to the oils on people's skin. Water alone can't wash them away. But soap has properties that attract it to both water and oil. Soap molecules have two different ends. One end is **hydrophilic**. It is drawn toward water. The other is **hydrophobic**. It is attracted to oil. When using soap and water to clean, the soap molecules grab both water and oil. When rinsed with water, both the soap and oils wash away.

Soap Molecules

Hydrophilic heads are attracted to water

Hydrophobic tails are attracted to oil

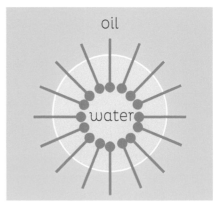

Making homemade soap was a time-consuming and messy process.

Pioneers made soap from leftover cooking grease and scraps of animal fat. They added lye, which was made by boiling ashes. They heated the fat and lye, along with lime from boiled animal bones, in large kettles over outdoor fires. Once the soap formed a soft mass, settlers allowed it to cool and harden. They then cut it into smaller pieces to use. Settlers could make enough soap in one day to last up to a year for their journey west.

SWEET AND SOUR

It's hard to imagine how the settlers fit all the gear and supplies they needed into a wagon. Besides food, soap, and medicine, they packed clothing, tools, and a lot of shoes. Settlers would wear out several pairs of shoes as they walked. They also brought tents, ropes, and feather beds.

Pioneers had to pack their wagons full of food, clothing, cookware, beds, tents, weapons, and everything else they would need to start a new life out West.

Settlers needed tools to help them along the trail and to build their new homes. They brought plows, saws, shovels, and axes. They also brought kettles and kegs for cooking and storing water and milk. They often kept two kegs for milk. One was for fresh milk to drink and one was for sour milk.

Sour milk is acidic. It tastes bad. But a trick of chemistry makes sour milk useful. It reacts chemically with baking soda. The reaction creates carbon dioxide gas bubbles. When baked in biscuits or pancakes, these bubbles make the food light and fluffy.

Settlers also packed a reflector oven. These ovens use radiant energy for baking. Heat radiating off a campfire bounces off the oven's shiny tin interior. It reflected onto the food inside to heat and bake it.

Sour milk was useful for baking fluffy biscuits and pancakes.

CHAPTER 3

HEADING OUT

Before the sun was up, a bugle blast marked the start of each day on the trail. The settlers loaded their wagons and began trudging across the vast plains. They traveled across land that is now Missouri, Kansas, Nebraska, Wyoming, and Idaho before reaching Oregon. The trail wound through the Rocky Mountains and Oregon's Blue Mountains.

The Oregon Trail followed rivers to have a source of fresh water. However, river crossings could be dangerous and difficult. Cows and oxen didn't want to swim. They had to be prodded to cross. River currents could pull people and animals underwater. Things such as stoves, trunks, and furniture were often left behind on river banks. They were too large or heavy to carry across the water.

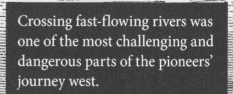

Crossing fast-flowing rivers was one of the most challenging and dangerous parts of the pioneers' journey west.

Pioneers often used **caulk** made with tar to fill holes in their wagons to float them like rafts across rivers. Caulking made wagons waterproof and **buoyant**. Buoyant things float because they are less dense than water. Density is how much matter is in an object for its size. As long as a wagon is mostly filled with air, it's less dense than water, so it floats. If water seeps in, it becomes denser than water and will sink.

HUNTING ON THE TRAIL

Many bison, elk, and deer roamed the western plains. Hunting parties set off from wagon trains to find food. Settlers brought rifles to hunt animals. These weapons used gunpowder to create a reaction in the rifle's bullet chamber. The gunpowder's combustive energy blasted the bullet through the rifle's chamber to hit its target.

Settlers used rifles to hunt bison, deer, and other animals for food.

How Rifles Work

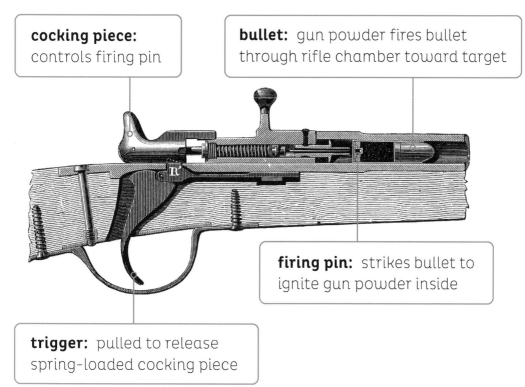

cocking piece: controls firing pin

bullet: gun powder fires bullet through rifle chamber toward target

firing pin: strikes bullet to ignite gun powder inside

trigger: pulled to release spring-loaded cocking piece

The science of gunpowder involves mixing a fuel with an oxidizer. An oxidizer is a chemical substance that contains oxygen. In gunpowder, charcoal and sulfur were used for fuel. Often potassium nitrate was used as an oxidizer. When mixed together, these ingredients have a lot of explosive energy.

Fact

Gunpowder was invented in China in the 800s AD. By the 1200s, the technology had made its way to Europe. European immigrants brought it to the United States.

NATURAL FUEL

Lunch on the trail was a welcome break for all. But to cook food, the pioneers needed to build fires. The plains had few trees or shrubs for firewood. So pioneers had to look for the next best thing. They found it in an unexpected form—poop! They gathered and burned piles of dried bison poop called buffalo chips. Bison were often called buffalo at the time. The animals had already eaten and processed the grasses and shrubs in their stomachs. The dry, compacted waste they left behind was useful for making campfires.

Jerky Making

Fresh meat was also preserved on the trail by making it into jerky. The settlers did this by hanging thin slices of meat over slow-burning fires. The smoke and heat removed the moisture in as little as a half a day. When dried, the jerky was ready to pack and stay safe from spoiling.

Each family brought cows for fresh milk. They drank the milk or used it to make butter. Fat molecules in fresh milk naturally separate. Milk fat, in the form of cream, floats to the top of the milk. This layer of cream is skimmed off. When shaken, the fat molecules clump together. These clumps become fresh butter. Pioneers often used butter churns to make butter. The churn was a wooden barrel with a hole in the top. A wooden stick in the hole was moved up and down to shake the cream and make butter. But butter churns weren't needed on the trail. Settlers hung containers of cream on their wagons instead. The wagons' jolting movements shook the cream to form fresh butter.

Butter churns were used to turn cream into fresh butter.

SAFE STOPS

Most wagon trains were led by a guide. He was usually an experienced traveler who knew the trail well. The guide figured out the speed of the animals and wagons and set the distance traveled each day. He decided where the wagon train would stop to camp for the evening. He also estimated when the travelers would reach forts along the trail. Forts were important for settlers on the trail. They could stop at the forts to rest and get supplies. But the supplies were often limited and costly.

Fur traders or the military built forts as places of trade or protection. Workers built forts from whatever material could be found nearby. In areas where trees were available, the forts were wooden.

In other places, such as Fort Laramie in Wyoming, the builders used adobe bricks. The bricks were stacked with mud for mortar to make the fort walls. Because adobe brick is a weak building material, the walls were thick and short.

Forts like Fort Laramie in Wyoming were important for settlers. People could safely rest and restock supplies behind a fort's strong walls.

Adobe bricks were made with a mixture of straw, sand, clay, and water.

CHAPTER 4

TRAIL DANGERS

Weather could be dangerous on the Oregon Trail. Storms and tornadoes popped up suddenly. A large section of the U.S. plains is nicknamed Tornado Alley. Tornadoes often occur there, usually in warm weather. These destructive twisters have winds of 40 to 318 miles (64 to 512 km) per hour. Powerful tornadoes can tear apart everything in their path.

Tornadoes form when hot, humid air is trapped below cool storm systems. When rain falls from the storms, the warm air rises into the cooler air. These updrafts of air can begin to spin and gain power. If these columns of spinning air touch the ground, they can leave a path of destruction.

cold air

strong wind

hot air

cloud of debris and dust

Powerful tornadoes often form on warm summer days over the grassy plains of the central United States.

The settlers couldn't do much about storms on the open plains. Taking shelter under their wagons was often their only option.

Fact
Dusty whirlwinds sometimes form like small tornadoes in dry areas. Some people call them dust devils. These mini tornadoes are usually weak and have wind speeds of less than 40 miles (64 km) per hour. They rarely cause damage.

DANGEROUS GERMS

In the 1800s, people didn't know what caused disease. They didn't understand that many diseases are caused by germs such as bacteria and viruses. Germs are microorganisms that live everywhere. Most aren't harmful. But people can be exposed to harmful germs by eating spoiled food, drinking unclean water, or by being near a sick person. These germs can multiply quickly. They attack healthy body cells to make people sick.

Pioneers on the Oregon Trail had no cures for disease. Measles, cholera, and diphtheria spread rapidly. These diseases are highly **contagious**. Measles causes fever, sore throat, and a nasty rash. Cholera causes diarrhea and severe dehydration. Diphtheria causes breathing problems. All can be deadly.

Today modern medicine can help prevent many deadly diseases. But the pioneers didn't have **vaccinations** and medicines like we have today. They used home remedies like castor oil, vinegar, and whiskey to treat illness and disease. But these treatments had little success. Many settlers died from disease along the trail.

Death Along the Trail

Many travelers died during the long journey on the Oregon Trail. Their families and friends didn't have much time to bury them. **Decomposition** starts just minutes after death. When cells no longer get oxygen, they turn acidic. Enzymes begin breaking them down immediately. These cell proteins start chemical reactions that cause a body to decay. For this reason, travelers often had to bury the dead in hasty graves along the trail. If they had time, they'd mark the grave with stones to remember their loved ones.

Graves of pioneers on the Oregon Trail in Wyoming

Accidents and serious injuries were a constant danger on the Oregon Trail.

Injuries also were a danger on the trail. Large animals and heavy wagons could crush people. Drownings at river crossings were common. Accidental shootings happened often. With unclean living conditions and no hospitals, injuries often led to more serious conditions.

Serious bacterial infections often caused tissue death. When body tissues near a wound die, it's called gangrene. The bacteria can quickly spread gangrene to healthy tissue throughout the body. It can infect internal organs, causing shock and death. In the 1800s, the only treatment was to cut away the dead tissue. To do this, pioneers used the only tools they had—butcher knives and saws.

Surgeries on the plains were bloody and painful. Few people survived them. The settlers had no **anesthesia** for these operations. Anesthesia numbs a person's nerves so pain messages aren't sent to the brain. It makes surgery less painful.

Stages of Gangrene Infection

Stage 1   **Stage 2**   **Stage 3**   **Stage 4**

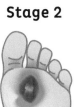

THE FIRST PEOPLE

The settlers weren't the first people to live in the western United States. Native people had lived on the land for centuries. Some were friendly to the settlers. Some were not. Others simply kept to themselves.

The settlers forever changed how the Native nations lived. Native people lived off the land. Many followed bison herds as they moved around on the plains. They ate bison meat and made clothing and shelters from the animals' hides. But as settlers moved west, they hunted the bison to the point that they almost died out. Many Native people went hungry or starved because their source of food was gone.

Many Native people also died from diseases that the settlers brought with them. Settlers had developed **antibodies** over the years to fight many diseases. But Native people didn't have these antibodies. The diseases quickly killed many of them.

Bison were an important source of food, clothing, and shelter for Native people living on the open plains.

Fact

The U.S. government forced many Native people to leave their land and live on reservations. These areas were usually on poor land that had few natural resources. Many Native people still live on reservations today.

CHAPTER 5

HITTING THE PASS

As the pioneers traveled, they looked for certain landmarks along the trail. The rock outcroppings and river crossings would guide them to South Pass in Wyoming. This pass was an important discovery. It made travel across the mountains possible. It is the lowest point in the Rocky Mountain range. It was the only place wagons could cross easily. Crossing the Rockies at any other point would be almost impossible. The terrain was rough. The mountain weather was harsh. Parts of the Rockies are covered with snow year-round.

Fact

Some parts of the Rocky Mountains get more than 400 inches (1,016 centimeters) of snow in a year.

Crossing through South Pass also meant crossing the Continental Divide. A continental divide separates the flow of water on a continent. The North American Continental Divide runs along the Rocky Mountains. All the rain that falls west of the divide flows west. All of the rivers eventually flow into the Pacific Ocean. All the rain and snow on the east side of the continental divide flows east. It ends up in the Atlantic Ocean or the Gulf of Mexico.

The Continental Divide

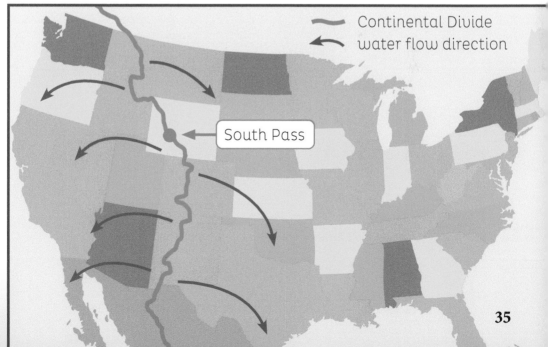

~ Continental Divide
← water flow direction

South Pass

BUBBLING WATERS

South Pass marked the halfway point on the trip west. It also led to an unexpected treat for the travelers. Not far beyond South Pass were the soda springs in Idaho.

The water in the springs is naturally **carbonated**. The springs were created by past volcanic activity. Beneath Earth's crust is a layer of melted rock called magma. Underground water is heated by magma and mixes with carbon dioxide gas. This gas makes the water bubbly and fizzy like soda.

Geysers erupt daily as part of the hot springs system at Soda Springs, Idaho.

The settlers found the water at the soda springs tasty. Some enjoyed bathing in it. They also washed clothes in the warm water. Some used it for cooking because the natural carbonation added airiness to baked goods. After the rough journey across the mountains, the wonders of the soda springs were a treat for the tired travelers.

How a Geyser Works

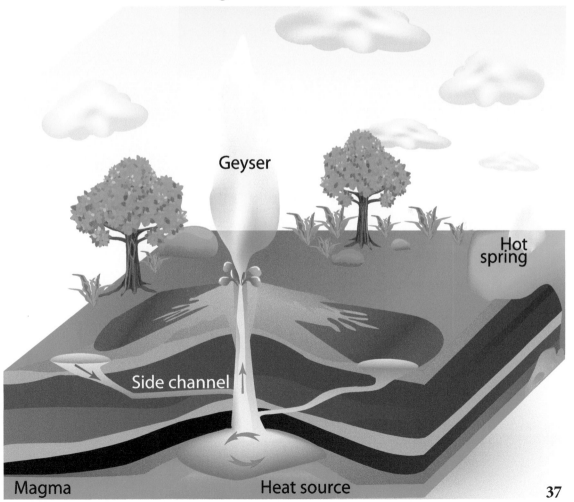

Geyser

Hot spring

Side channel

Magma

Heat source

CHAPTER 6

OFF THE BEATEN PATH

After making their way through South Pass, travelers still had a long journey. It was about 1,000 more miles (1,600 km) to the Oregon Territory. But some broke off to take the Mormon Trail. It led to Salt Lake City in Utah. Others took the California Trail. Many settlers chose to seek out riches in gold in California instead of going to Oregon.

Gold is a rare chemical element. It's prized for its beauty and ability to be formed into valuable objects like jewelry. Over thousands of years, earthquakes and volcanoes brought some of the gold in Earth's mantle to the surface. As rocks eroded over time, gold appeared. Most of it was found underground. Miners worked hard to drill into the ground and dig out the gold.

Some gold washed into rivers and streams. Miners used gravity to pan for gold. They scooped sand and rocks into a metal pan with a flat bottom. They then shook the pan under water. Sand washed off into the stream. The heavier materials, such as gold flakes or nuggets, settled to the bottom of the pan. The miners could then pick out any gold they found.

Fact

Gold was discovered in California in 1848. It sparked a huge surge of people coming to California that later became known as the Gold Rush.

KEEPING HYDRATED

For Oregon travelers, the journey got easier after the South Pass. But for those heading to California, the worst was yet to come. They still had to cross the Great Basin Desert and the Sierra Nevada mountain range. They faced temperature extremes that often affected their ability to find water and animals to hunt.

Humans can survive for several weeks without food. But water is another story. Sixty percent of the human body is made of water. All the body's systems depend on it to function. Every living cell is partly water. Water also lubricates people's joints, helps maintain body temperature, and helps flush waste from the body. People can survive only about three days without water.

Travelers faced another danger in the mountains. The higher they climbed, the colder the temperatures became. Heavy snow usually covers the Sierra Nevada mountains from October through June. Extreme cold can cause hypothermia—a very low body temperature. When a person's body temperature drops below 95°F (35°C), the body's systems begin to slow down. Death can follow unless a person warms up.

The Donner Party

Most pioneers who headed to California tried to cross the Sierra Nevada range before October to avoid snowstorms. But one group, the Donner Party, got trapped by winter weather in 1846–47. The settlers were unable to cross the mountains before heavy snow made the crossing impossible. Only 47 of the 87 members of the Donner Party survived the winter. Those who survived did so by eating the bodies of their dead companions until they were rescued.

GOING UPHILL

Getting wagons and supplies over hills and riverbanks wasn't an easy task. And moving them over the mountains was nearly impossible. But settlers found solutions in nature to help them move their wagons up steep mountain slopes. Attaching one end of a rope to a wagon and the other end around the trunk of a tree worked similarly to a pulley. This simple machine changes the direction of a force, which makes it easier to lift things.

Moving wagons up steep mountain sides was a major challenge.

Other travelers wrapped a rope over a log on the edge of the hill. When objects rub together, they create a force called friction. A smooth log has much less friction than a rocky ledge does. The reduced friction meant the rope could easily slide over the log. This method made it much easier to pull the wagon up the hill.

Wagon-Lifting Devices

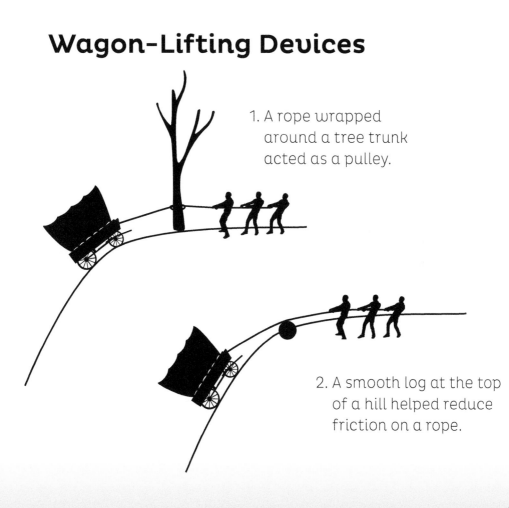

1. A rope wrapped around a tree trunk acted as a pulley.

2. A smooth log at the top of a hill helped reduce friction on a rope.

THE END
OF THE TRAIL

After months of hardship, the journey was over. The settlers had reached their new homes on the West Coast. But how would they get word to families back east?

The Pony Express carried messages across the United States from April 1860 to October 1861. The Pony Express used single riders on horseback. They traded off messages at relay stations. Riders could deliver a message from the West Coast to Missouri in an average of 10 days. Heavy stagecoaches took about 25 days to make the same trip. However, the Pony Express couldn't beat new technology.

In October 1861, the Western Union Company finished the transcontinental telegraph line. The telegraph sent messages through wires using electricity. Messages were sent using Morse code. This code uses electronic dots and dashes for each letter of the alphabet. The telegraph was a miracle of science at the time. It could send a message across hundreds of miles almost instantly.

Before telegraphs and railroads crossed the country, the Pony Express and stagecoaches carried messages and people across the West.

In 1869, the Transcontinental Railroad was completed. It connected to railroads in the eastern United States. Suddenly, people could travel across the country in days instead of months. The railroad's completion signaled the end of the Oregon Trail. But westward expansion was first possible because of the brave pioneers on the Oregon Trail. These settlers used courage and science to survive a dangerous journey and start new lives in the West.

GLOSSARY

anesthesia (a-nuhs-THEE-zhuh)—a gas or injection that prevents pain during medical treatments and surgeries

antibody (AN-ti-bah-dee)—a substance produced by white blood cells that fights infections and disease

buoyant (BOI-uhnt)—able to float on water

carbonated (KAR-buh-nay-tuhd)—something that contains carbon dioxide gas

caulk (KAWK)—a waterproof paste applied to a hole to keep water out

contagious (kuhn-TAY-juhss)—something easily spread from one person to another

decomposition (dee-kohm-puh-ZIH-shuhn)—process of decaying

element (E-luh-muhnt)—a substance that cannot be broken down into simpler substances

hydrophilic (hye-druh-FIH-lik)—something that attracts water

hydrophobic (hy-druh-FOH-bik)—something that repels water

microorganism (mye-kroh-OR-gan-iz-uhm)—a living thing that is too small to see without a microscope

molecule (MOL-uh-kyool)—a group of atoms with specific properties

polymer (POL-uh-mur)—tiny pieces of matter that are linked together; polymers can be natural or human-made

vaccination (vak-suh-NAY-shun)—a shot of medicine that protects from a disease

READ MORE

Gibson, Karen Bush. *The Oregon Trail: The Journey Across the Country From Lewis and Clark to the Transcontinental Railroad With 25 Projects*. White River Junction, VT: Nomad Press, 2017.

Loh-Hagan, Virginia. *Heading West: Oregon Trail and Westward Expansion*. Ann Arbor, MI: Cherry Lake Publishing, 2019.

Rusick, Jessica. *Enduring the Oregon Trail: A This or That Debate*. North Mankato, MN: Capstone Press, 2020.

Russo, Kristin. *Viewpoints on the Oregon Trail and Westward Expansion*. Ann Arbor, MI: Cherry Lake Publishing, 2018.

INTERNET SITES

9 Things You May Not Know About the Oregon Trail
www.history.com/news/9-things-you-may-not-know-about-the-oregon-trail

The Oregon Trail for Kids and Teachers
westernexpansion.mrdonn.org/oregontrail.html

Westward Expansion: Oregon Trail
www.ducksters.com/history/westward_expansion/oregon_trail.php

INDEX